Improve Your Vocabulary

Enriching Word Power the Fun Way

V&S PUBLISHERS

Published by:

V&S PUBLISHERS

F-2/16, Ansari Road, Daryaganj, New Delhi-110002
☎ 011-23240026, 011-23240027 • *Fax:* 011-23240028
Email: info@vspublishers.com • *Website:* www.vspublishers.com

Branch : Hyderabad
5-1-707/1, Brij Bhawan (Beside Central Bank of India Lane)
Bank Street, Koti, Hyderabad - 500 095
☎ 040-24737290
E-mail: vspublishershyd@gmail.com

ISBN 978-93-505708-0-7
Edition 2014

Printed at : Param Offsetters, Okhla, New Delhi-110020

Publisher's Note

It has been our prime motto and a constant endeavour at **V&S Publishers** to publish books of **Value** and **Substance** from the time of its inception. With a backlist of **about 350 titles** to our credit, it's a great pleasure to inform all our esteemed readers that we have come up with this altogether exclusive series of books on **English language and its various usage** called the **EXC-EL Series or the Excellent English Learning Series**.

The series contains a set of books on *various usage of* Words and Phrases in English, the significance of Grammar, correct Pronunciation, etc., called *English Grammar And Usage, English Vocabulary made Easy, Improve Your Vocabulary* and *Spoken English* to enhance and enrich your vocabulary, increase your command over the language and make you more confident and fluent in your day to day conversations, written and verbal interactions, etc.

The present book, ***Improve Your Vocabulary*** is a unique book in itself, particularly meant for the school children, in the age group of 7 to 14 years. In this book, students can playfully learn to complete the words in **Word Search Puzzles** with the given clues, **Unjumble Words** to create meaningful words, learn about *Antonyms, Synonyms, Homonyms* and *Homophones, Prefixes* and *Suffixes, Idioms, Proverbs and*

Phrases, etc., through the **brief explanations** given in the book along with **several small, simple and interesting exercises**.

Hence friends, the book is ideal for all the school kids *who wish to learn the language and enhance their vocabulary – the fun way,* without getting bored, tensed or tired. This is the main idea behind publishing the book and hope it serves its purpose well.

Contents

Introduction

A person's vocabulary consists of the set of words within a language that he/she is familiar with. With age and education, vocabulary usually develops, serving as a useful and important fundamental tool for acquiring knowledge and communication. Acquiring an extensive vocabulary is a trait which always serves as an advantage to a person even though one faces challenges in the process of learning. Vocabulary is widely defined as "all the words used and known by a particular person."

However, just knowing a word does not simply refer to being able to recognise or use it. There are several aspects attached to one's word knowledge which are used to measure the efficiency of the word knowledge. The words we understand to communicate effectively can be referred to our vocabulary. The best way one can present his/her communication skills and expressions is through his/her extensive vocabulary.

Everyone whether a beginner in English to the veterans in English and Journalism, are all aware of the frustration of not having the right word available immediately in that lexicon. At times, it's a matter of not being able to recall the right word and sometimes, we never know it. It is also saddening when one reads a newspaper or homework assignment and comes across words whose meanings elude us.

English is a vast language and will always have scope of expansion through vocabulary, with new words coming in every other day. People from all walks of life, including those with the most advanced of vocabularies usually come across words that they don't know. Many a time, this leaves us with a sense of awkwardness or confusion as to what was spoken or written and one has to overcome this.

In today's competitive world, just acquiring the bookish knowledge is not enough. One has to go out and out to present himself/herself in the best and the most unique way. There is nothing better than an impressive conversation because it always works. A powerful and intellectual conversation leaves a great impact on others leaving you with many doors open for numerous opportunities in life. Whether it's on a school level or business level, a good command over a language will always be an add on to one's persona and a great advantage. A good command over any language comes naturally when one is good with words. Word knowledge always helps build stronger vocabulary and as hard as it sounds, it's quite easier than that.

The knowledge of Vocabulary must be as deep as it is wide. The book aims in enhancing the readers' vocabulary not just by the addition of a sheer number of words children eventually acquire, but also by developing an understanding of the word base they already have. The depth of word knowledge vastly depends on a child's understanding of the concepts that a word represents, a word with different meanings, associations the word evokes, how a word is used in conjunction with other words, grammar (how a word behaves in a sentence) with the other words that sound like it, etc. Keeping all these in mind, the book has been designed in such a way that it covers mostly all the various activities which will help boost the readers' confidence about their vocabulary.

Language is basically used to express our intentions, put forward our feelings, and understand the ideas of others. **'Word knowledge'** being the most critical piece of language development makes it important for people to comprehend the words and their meanings as they make the basis of the language. Children who have a wider exposure and acquire good vocabulary skills are often able to think more deeply, express themselves in an intellectual manner, and grasp new things more quickly. This knowledge gives the children an upper hand as they are also very likely to be successful not only in learning to read, but also in initiating worthy and intellectual conversations. A child's thoughts become more reliant on his/her ability to self-express in a gesture-free and babble-free manner.

Children automatically build interest as the book is not just another boring storybook full of theory. It helps children learn in a more interesting and playful manner. The exercises require brainstorming which keeps the children on toes. Through this book, the reader will actively learn and obtain a richer vocabulary in less time. It helps the reader use the required vocabulary tools in the most effective manner to work out word meanings which further equips the reader with the right word knowledge. On an optimistic note, the book serves various methods for working out these word meanings and to improve one's vocabulary. They are not difficult and anyone can put them into practice in one's day to day life, whether it is verbal or written communication, and thus, improve one's knowledge and vocabulary in English.

The framework of this book has been designed in such a manner that it keeps the reader holding on to it without making him/her feel bored or monotonous. This introduction will help the reader understand the concept of the book which emphasises on the importance of vocabulary, especially in the contemporary world.

Basically, the aim of this book is to make the learning process easy and exciting, and at the same time, helping people learn new and difficult words in a playful and interesting way. The positive approach taken for this book is to encourage this fun learning process which helps keep peoples' brains on a move and constantly working towards enhancing the word knowledge.

This introduction of the book is followed by various types of exercises based on the different aspects of English vocabulary which have different relationships with other words, such as *synonyms*, *antonyms*, *homophones*, *homonyms*, *acronyms*, etc. There are multiple exercises based on different topics in order to increase the word knowledge on a wider scale. Each topic has a different exercise with a description given before it as to how to go about it, the relevant words and meanings associated with the exercise and all the necessary details needed. The standard remains generalised for everyone to access the book and make good use of it. The exercises are meant to be a notch higher in order to make learning more effective and efficient. Every question has an elaborated answer at the back of the book for the readers' convenience.

The book encourages the readers to develop their vocabulary through active working, word meanings and several other exercises. The reader is expected not to try and rush to the reference materials and rather analyse the word and discover the meanings on their own first. This will not only help give the reader self-confidence, but will also support long-term retention. This learning process makes the reader come out of the comfort zone where he has to apply his/her vocabulary skills and not just sit back on the couch reading the book.

WORD SEARCH

The *word search puzzle* –also known as *word seek, word find*, etc –was initially designed by *Norman E. Gibat* in the *Selenby Digest on March 1, 1968 in Norman, Oklahoma.* Soon this idea of Gibat spread across the place and the puzzle became locally very popular and many started following it. Word search is still very famous among the teachers and students and even the daily newspapers for its smart approach towards learning and finding new words.

A word search puzzle is a word game comprising letters of a word in a grid, that is usually rectangular or square shaped. The main objective of this *word game* is to find all the hidden words inside the box. The words may be placed *vertically* –both *backward* and *forward, horizontally* –both upward and downward or the word might be written upside down and diagonally. Many times, a list of hidden words is provided along with the puzzle to make it more challenging and interesting. One has to find the hidden words by himself/ herself without the help of the list of hidden words. More often than not, this *word search puzzle* is based on a theme and all the hidden words are related to this theme. To make it easier for the player, a clue is given for every hidden word and the rest is for the player to figure out.

The best strategy to find the hidden words is to first look

row by row –both *forward* and *backward* –just so that no word is missed and then column by column both upward and downward and diagonally. This way the player goes through the whole puzzle –vertically, horizontally and diagonally which enables the reader to spot the words comfortably. In case the list of hidden words is given, it becomes all the more easy to spot the word by the initial alphabet of the given word.

Given below is an example of how a word search puzzle looks like. The puzzle may not necessarily be arranged in the same manner, or it may not contain the same letters.

For Example:

H	G	S	H	E	A	U	A	T	E
N	R	P	A	T	O	E	O	W	G
I	A	E	L	I	M	E	M	A	Y
P	V	E	F	L	O	W	E	R	S
A	E	C	M	R	N	H	V	F	D
R	S	H	A	I	D	O	D	L	E
A	N	E	S	I	A	N	H	A	T
D	T	S	T	G	Y	O	L	G	I
E	N	M	E	M	O	R	I	A	L
S	R	E	M	E	M	B	E	R	C

Exercise

The last line of this puzzle has the word, 'member' written horizontally.

1. Find the words given below in the crossword puzzle and encircle them.

H	A	Y	E	C	L	V	O	F	D	Y	J	M
O	F	Q	D	G	Q	C	F	O	E	N	E	P
N	F	W	K	R	F	B	M	M	G	O	H	L
T	E	M	K	U	A	I	T	T	P	M	H	U
E	C	M	F	I	N	P	O	Q	T	R	P	E
T	T	Y	S	A	C	I	O	N	H	A	X	X
D	I	Q	T	W	R	J	U	E	K	H	E	N
E	O	E	F	T	G	B	O	I	J	G	F	U
R	N	N	A	M	U	S	I	N	G	V	A	X
D	L	P	E	V	S	Z	C	A	O	I	L	T
Y	P	S	D	H	S	I	N	I	M	I	D	Q
E	E	L	W	I	O	W	F	A	S	F	C	T
L	H	H	B	W	C	U	X	T	Q	U	I	I

AFFECTION	HARMONY	DOMINATE
JEOPARDY	AMUSING	MEMBER
PATRIOT	DIMINISH	

2. Find the words given below in the crossword puzzle and encircle them.

F	C	H	A	S	E	R	H	T	B	E	T	B
L	R	U	Q	O	Z	Y	E	D	L	G	K	R
A	G	W	C	T	P	M	W	E	D	W	X	U
M	O	V	X	N	O	I	S	U	L	L	I	T
B	W	R	T	T	Y	T	O	U	J	G	L	R
O	E	I	I	D	A	S	U	O	C	O	O	E
Y	O	P	Q	B	N	I	A	N	C	F	B	P
A	E	Y	L	B	W	R	M	T	R	T	Z	Y
N	K	I	K	X	X	S	E	X	N	E	F	Z
T	S	U	T	Z	J	P	X	G	R	A	R	R
H	Y	S	K	K	D	H	R	T	Z	M	F	Y
P	R	T	J	U	Z	N	J	L	M	V	E	B
W	M	Y	M	L	I	X	M	C	Q	S	H	E

CHASE	EPITOME	ESTABLISH
FANTASY	FLAMBOYANT	ILLUSION
PERTURB		

3. **Find the words given below in the crossword puzzle and encircle them.**

I	R	W	G	J	S	S	V	M	H	H	L	M
E	E	E	Y	N	R	I	V	H	L	S	X	U
Q	Y	A	V	S	Z	R	V	T	A	I	L	K
E	Z	I	N	I	T	U	R	C	S	N	R	K
T	V	O	O	D	V	A	H	P	Y	E	L	U
W	E	K	V	U	Y	E	F	F	M	L	Z	D
F	P	R	Q	N	O	M	I	W	R	P	X	A
I	M	F	P	Q	H	L	N	R	J	E	R	W
C	N	R	W	R	P	K	S	W	B	R	S	J
K	K	G	X	M	E	P	I	V	O	T	A	L
L	Y	H	E	V	R	T	I	Q	S	N	N	U
E	E	X	P	F	L	M	N	F	A	D	J	E
M	E	V	A	Z	Z	D	G	I	J	X	E	S

EXEMPLIFY FICKLE INTERPRET

PIVOTAL REPLENISH REVIVE

SCRUTINIZE

4. **Find the words given below in the crossword puzzle and encircle them.**

H	B	E	V	N	N	J	R	R	I	W	A	E
A	A	G	N	T	Y	R	E	L	N	O	D	R
O	H	L	A	I	K	D	U	V	G	Y	J	O
F	Y	A	L	Z	L	C	W	U	E	D	X	D
W	U	L	L	U	R	C	L	B	N	W	H	A
Q	F	K	C	A	C	I	N	O	I	Z	Y	G
V	D	R	T	T	P	I	P	I	O	F	P	T
L	E	I	L	U	M	W	N	K	U	M	H	T
B	V	W	P	F	F	O	Y	A	S	J	S	I
E	D	A	U	S	R	E	P	B	T	C	K	M
Z	Q	P	O	G	V	K	F	I	O	I	H	Q
Z	W	Y	I	E	U	Y	D	P	I	F	O	V
H	K	W	R	O	E	C	Q	B	S	N	I	N

ADORE HALLUCINATION NCLINE

INGENIOUS LUCRATIVE PUPIL

5. Find the words given below in the crossword puzzle and encircle them.

S	D	P	M	R	U	W	Z	B	C	X	Z	R
P	E	P	Q	B	A	R	D	C	Q	S	P	A
Y	L	K	Y	D	T	T	Y	Q	U	P	S	G
S	I	G	B	Y	N	M	I	O	Q	S	D	N
P	C	V	G	D	E	B	I	O	A	V	L	I
N	A	S	G	A	M	C	K	U	N	G	Z	V
H	T	Y	G	K	A	N	L	S	V	A	E	C
Q	E	L	H	U	R	T	V	G	I	W	L	V
L	L	J	Q	T	E	N	D	E	N	C	Y	X
R	N	O	I	U	P	B	V	J	X	C	Q	I
C	L	N	P	U	M	A	J	Q	P	E	C	T
D	A	O	P	E	E	I	M	S	Q	V	Q	L
B	D	I	W	R	T	E	G	A	G	N	E	W

ASSAULT DELICATE ENGAGE

LOQUACIOUS RATIONAL TEMPERAMENT

TENDENCY

6. **Locate the words given below in this crossword puzzle and encircle them.**

Q	W	N	H	V	E	T	F	N	A	L	X	Q
P	J	Q	X	T	O	S	D	L	B	A	T	V
Q	B	N	I	E	F	N	L	U	B	U	E	P
Q	T	I	S	Z	T	E	Y	H	L	T	E	N
C	I	T	A	M	G	A	R	P	U	R	F	P
C	Z	R	C	A	F	T	U	C	Z	I	M	K
I	M	C	T	M	Q	H	E	Q	N	V	D	G
G	M	I	Q	V	E	X	M	E	E	Y	V	W
B	O	P	I	V	E	S	I	L	D	D	D	K
N	M	M	O	X	B	A	F	F	L	E	A	R
V	B	R	H	S	T	I	A	A	K	E	I	R
Y	J	M	M	C	E	C	U	C	U	Z	R	G
C	A	Y	J	K	H	R	W	B	G	K	Z	U

ADEQUATE ALLEGATION BAFFLE

EXECUTE IMPOSE PRAGMATIC

VIRTUAL

7. **Find the words given below in the word search and encircle them.**

X	N	Z	J	J	Y	B	A	E	C	E	F	D
H	O	X	B	D	A	U	X	O	V	N	L	H
A	I	F	E	V	M	P	A	I	N	V	N	Z
V	T	Q	I	G	L	E	S	E	C	C	L	F
O	A	B	M	O	D	N	A	R	L	T	W	P
R	V	S	R	G	E	P	P	A	E	I	B	R
V	O	E	A	F	M	L	Y	U	S	P	F	E
A	N	C	F	B	L	A	W	G	K	C	U	V
D	N	O	B	N	O	X	I	O	U	S	X	E
K	I	V	H	P	W	T	A	H	E	N	C	N
K	F	T	Q	M	G	Y	A	E	J	G	K	T
X	D	E	E	I	Y	X	Q	G	E	X	L	W
Z	I	G	R	F	C	W	L	I	E	M	T	T

EXPLORE INNOVATION OBNOXIOUS

OFFENSIVE PREVENT RANDOM

SABOTAGE

8. Locate and Encircle the words written below in the given word search.

Y	J	C	T	O	H	U	S	K	H	M	R	V
K	R	N	O	E	H	S	S	S	Q	U	E	W
H	E	A	X	N	N	L	I	W	L	L	V	A
P	J	I	R	R	C	N	F	D	N	U	E	Q
T	M	W	Y	O	E	I	E	K	S	C	N	R
J	A	K	F	L	P	C	S	Z	N	I	G	D
X	G	S	P	T	R	M	E	E	O	R	E	Q
A	Q	E	X	Q	F	S	E	D	V	R	E	I
A	R	G	X	I	Q	B	F	T	B	U	R	M
E	N	G	R	A	V	E	W	P	N	C	D	C
O	D	T	P	B	T	C	F	S	J	O	F	V
B	E	Q	E	C	J	J	T	W	M	Z	C	Q
M	A	F	H	O	A	U	Z	X	D	G	N	E

CONCISE CONTEMPORARY CURRICULUM

ENGRAVE FETCH REPLENISH

REVENGE

9. **Locate and encircle the words given below and solve the crossword puzzle.**

R	E	K	U	H	L	W	G	K	T	C	E	A
E	C	T	M	Y	Z	A	E	W	G	A	S	B
T	Q	A	A	R	E	T	I	R	E	B	N	A
Z	Z	W	B	I	R	A	Q	H	R	L	E	T
H	S	K	H	W	L	A	L	Q	R	Y	C	E
T	N	E	M	R	I	A	P	M	I	J	I	F
D	B	I	V	P	U	W	T	R	W	Z	L	K
F	B	G	M	T	N	J	C	E	T	L	S	D
P	B	M	C	P	H	E	S	R	R	H	Q	C
K	R	A	B	H	A	L	W	Q	G	C	Y	Y
H	F	E	A	V	H	C	M	R	I	L	G	Z
V	X	B	B	O	L	V	T	V	E	D	H	B
X	S	J	R	R	U	E	E	M	R	B	M	E

ABATE FACTUAL IMPACT

IMPAIRMENT LICENSE RETALIATE

RETIRE

10. **Find the words given below in the word search and encircle them.**

U	Q	C	P	K	C	Z	G	K	T	G	K	Q
S	S	I	N	M	U	K	E	K	C	S	U	Y
R	U	M	A	V	T	H	P	W	I	T	Z	Z
U	B	O	G	J	S	I	K	K	R	U	Y	J
S	U	O	M	I	N	A	N	U	T	H	X	M
F	N	K	D	A	O	V	Z	C	S	F	X	I
M	E	D	E	P	F	B	V	S	E	W	K	T
E	A	C	F	D	W	N	S	P	R	I	J	V
F	B	C	P	P	T	M	I	C	M	G	D	N
A	V	P	O	P	U	L	A	R	E	Z	N	T
U	P	B	C	A	J	Q	A	S	M	N	F	W
T	Z	G	O	J	Z	W	C	Y	G	J	E	W
Z	Z	U	Y	Q	R	D	Y	A	P	F	M	J

FADDISH INFAMOUS NAG

OBSCENE POPULAR RESTRICT

UNANIMOUS

11. Locate the words written below in the word search.

W	S	B	G	B	I	Q	S	M	U	B	V	K
R	U	U	H	A	C	Y	U	J	E	Z	T	P
C	R	A	B	X	O	N	O	T	G	R	J	J
E	O	Y	P	K	N	S	E	X	L	N	T	U
R	S	N	K	X	I	G	N	S	J	U	B	X
S	N	R	S	X	C	A	E	M	D	W	C	P
R	H	P	A	O	W	N	G	P	A	A	X	H
T	R	L	C	F	L	Z	O	T	Y	W	P	N
B	N	C	X	R	N	E	M	N	M	O	D	G
Z	F	B	B	W	R	N	O	C	I	P	E	L
N	L	H	F	K	S	B	H	G	O	W	E	Q
S	A	C	R	I	F	I	C	E	L	A	K	C
Y	E	E	I	Q	G	Z	B	E	Q	Y	A	G

ABYSS	CONSOLE	CULT
EPIC	HOMOGENEOUS	ICONIC
SACRIFICE		

12. Can you Find and encircle the words in the word search given below?

N	A	D	I	F	L	A	O	I	A	C	R	R
Z	O	T	A	K	C	Z	H	S	N	E	C	E
P	U	I	Z	N	J	T	T	U	T	B	H	D
E	K	U	T	J	G	O	O	T	P	I	A	N
R	G	Z	A	U	N	E	U	I	F	O	L	U
J	G	V	U	I	A	Q	R	X	S	T	L	L
C	V	K	S	S	L	C	E	O	J	Y	E	B
O	S	H	N	Q	J	V	Q	F	U	E	N	A
E	R	I	P	S	N	I	G	V	A	S	G	O
T	F	J	G	R	O	D	T	H	X	V	E	S
K	P	B	T	N	Y	E	A	B	N	G	P	Z
C	K	Q	S	M	Y	H	B	Y	L	I	O	N
K	N	G	E	P	T	G	G	N	Y	Z	H	A

ASTONISH BLUNDER CAUTION

CHALLENGE DANGEROUS INSPIRE

UTTER

13. Look for the words given below and encircle them.

C	Z	T	L	H	W	S	R	H	R	E	H	Q
V	E	V	E	L	Q	E	V	E	U	U	T	B
Y	P	G	O	G	E	D	N	T	I	H	U	P
Q	P	S	Y	K	D	K	H	E	L	O	O	A
C	I	O	R	E	H	A	M	R	G	W	Y	L
T	O	U	G	H	N	A	G	O	E	P	Y	K
C	V	H	L	A	L	E	H	G	B	S	N	Y
N	N	Y	S	B	N	K	J	E	G	A	T	V
P	H	I	F	X	G	X	C	N	K	L	H	D
A	A	T	E	F	V	K	E	E	M	E	A	U
T	O	O	H	Y	Z	P	M	O	Y	M	Q	Z
V	V	X	K	A	O	K	F	U	W	G	W	L
P	B	L	A	J	M	F	W	S	N	H	I	Y

BLAME	EUTHANASIA	GADGET
HEROIC	HETEROGENEOUS	TOUGH
YOUTH		

14. Exercise your brain a little to find the words given below in this crossword puzzle.

A	A	L	H	Z	G	S	Y	A	F	N	N	P
B	Q	N	O	L	A	C	E	W	F	D	O	I
A	Z	N	U	Z	D	S	J	X	L	O	Y	Q
G	L	P	V	Q	D	K	I	N	B	P	N	D
C	O	L	L	A	B	O	R	A	T	E	O	Y
K	X	R	E	K	H	X	T	C	X	M	M	F
N	K	A	G	G	P	R	E	V	H	B	E	J
C	P	W	E	K	A	R	Y	M	O	A	G	Q
A	Z	D	A	Z	E	T	E	N	J	R	E	T
S	T	K	V	M	H	V	I	U	Q	R	H	Y
R	W	X	O	W	Z	F	L	O	A	A	S	T
X	N	N	P	B	H	Y	B	T	N	S	B	Y
E	Y	N	O	I	S	A	C	C	O	S	L	F

ALLEGATION CEREMONY COLLABORATE

EMBARRASS HEGEMONY OCCASION

TABOO

15. Locate the words given below and solve the crossword puzzle.

K	I	Y	N	O	Y	A	F	U	F	R	P	E
S	B	N	J	O	K	C	L	B	E	H	U	B
Q	X	U	T	Q	I	F	Y	G	Q	E	G	I
A	W	A	E	Z	N	T	E	S	R	U	A	R
O	D	C	M	T	T	N	A	U	R	F	C	C
U	P	Q	P	K	E	F	T	V	O	L	K	S
I	W	R	T	R	O	L	N	U	L	M	K	B
O	K	X	A	M	U	H	G	K	J	A	V	U
M	J	T	T	C	T	M	N	U	D	H	S	S
I	E	S	I	E	R	U	T	N	E	V	D	A
N	W	P	O	F	L	A	C	H	I	E	V	E
E	S	C	N	G	T	H	T	O	H	P	F	B
F	S	N	P	R	L	E	H	U	V	D	E	Z

ACHIEVE ADVENTURE CULTURE

REGENERATE SALVATION SUBSCRIBE

TEMPTATION

16. **Exercise your brain a little to find the words given below in this word search.**

Y	I	X	M	K	R	U	I	X	P	O	H	N
D	N	E	F	F	O	P	T	Y	O	U	L	I
E	X	F	X	C	V	I	I	K	R	Y	H	A
Y	V	O	Y	F	O	J	W	D	T	K	Q	V
X	A	E	V	D	R	M	L	I	I	N	R	M
S	W	G	I	H	C	E	P	P	O	P	O	P
P	L	A	L	R	M	Q	W	O	N	V	C	X
U	A	S	O	R	G	C	Q	Q	U	G	J	F
E	E	K	X	U	G	I	S	R	Z	N	G	U
O	P	P	O	R	T	U	N	I	T	Y	D	K
J	V	H	K	T	J	R	Q	J	Z	W	F	O
B	B	P	S	X	P	X	I	U	A	M	C	C
P	U	O	S	T	J	W	X	E	H	S	C	X

COMPOUND GRIEVE HURDLE

OFFEND OPPORTUNITY PORTION

VAIN

17. **Locate the words given below and solve the word search.**

X	N	Z	V	B	N	W	Q	A	G	D	V	W
S	Y	W	N	X	I	D	O	T	D	W	B	N
L	A	V	O	R	P	P	A	L	E	P	O	D
Y	G	R	T	L	W	L	B	S	L	V	E	U
T	E	X	T	E	N	T	U	A	K	A	V	P
E	I	O	K	F	E	F	Q	X	F	Z	H	G
I	N	B	E	V	F	G	M	F	X	F	U	S
R	U	R	P	I	T	M	Q	X	E	J	L	F
A	K	A	D	E	R	D	X	Y	E	C	N	E
V	W	L	I	Y	E	P	N	V	J	T	B	I
B	L	U	Y	V	N	M	Z	R	C	M	T	P
W	R	X	V	H	D	O	B	E	A	F	T	P
P	F	Z	O	Y	S	C	S	K	U	Q	X	V

APPROVAL BAFFLE DIFFUSE

EXTENT SHALLOW TREND

VARIETY

18. Can you solve the following crossword by locating the words given below?

E	P	G	T	R	Z	M	E	E	I	R	F	U
C	V	R	U	I	Y	K	T	W	A	O	G	B
O	G	A	K	W	M	A	S	D	X	R	H	Z
N	U	G	L	D	N	D	I	B	C	C	T	V
F	A	Z	I	U	A	C	A	A	I	R	C	T
E	O	X	T	M	A	N	D	A	T	O	R	Y
S	T	R	V	L	L	T	A	E	M	X	R	J
S	O	P	V	M	Q	Z	E	I	H	O	V	I
F	U	W	Q	A	P	Y	A	A	F	K	D	N
L	Y	F	I	C	A	P	T	C	R	C	R	V
J	W	F	Y	C	L	J	F	I	W	Z	X	U
G	W	P	F	Q	W	G	J	C	V	K	E	G
B	T	D	T	S	U	E	E	X	B	M	K	H

ADMIT CONFESS EVALUATE

FORTUNATE MANDATORY PACIFY

RADICAL

19. Solve the following crossword by locating the words given below.

I	L	D	S	I	V	Y	E	C	U	B	E	P
C	P	J	U	Q	N	T	T	I	S	O	T	G
X	E	R	T	A	A	R	Y	T	E	K	L	P
T	J	O	E	T	M	V	H	E	N	N	O	Z
D	O	C	I	D	Y	V	W	H	H	C	G	E
E	J	D	C	Z	I	D	T	T	A	M	L	E
Q	E	U	T	S	T	C	K	A	N	C	I	P
M	W	O	R	R	O	S	T	P	C	F	O	R
A	P	P	R	A	I	S	E	A	E	N	T	I
Q	E	I	U	V	A	Q	L	M	D	T	M	Y
E	F	S	R	S	Q	U	M	E	L	I	I	P
I	D	W	G	R	O	I	R	Y	P	X	C	N
L	S	U	E	O	O	E	R	H	U	G	C	I

APATHETIC	APPRAISE	ENHANCE
MEDITATE	PONDER	PREDICT
SORROW		

20. Solve the following word search by locating the words given below.

L	I	G	R	Q	A	E	T	W	D	D	T	Y
Q	Q	T	N	L	L	U	Q	I	N	N	X	L
O	J	B	G	I	U	W	S	Y	J	U	F	Q
U	X	R	R	G	N	D	L	U	U	O	T	O
P	F	E	G	W	A	R	R	C	M	F	R	U
N	T	H	N	I	R	M	A	O	L	N	D	C
S	C	W	N	A	Z	B	F	E	O	O	X	S
B	B	F	R	Z	U	M	O	P	Y	C	Y	L
B	U	O	P	P	O	S	E	A	U	W	G	Z
L	B	E	B	N	Y	L	B	N	S	C	O	F
S	U	T	S	A	P	O	V	H	D	T	E	U
G	N	I	L	L	A	P	P	A	J	G	Z	D
F	M	N	F	G	Q	J	Z	I	S	Q	Y	J

APPALLING BOAST CONFOUND

DISDAINFUL OPPOSE STERILE

YEARNING

JUMBLED WORDS

The concept of jumbled words was first created by *Martin Naydel in 1954*. This word game is based on testing one's smartness through arranging the jumbled words in order to form meaningful *anagrams*. This word game is also very popular with school kids and teachers as it helps build a strong sense of word spellings. This not only helps one to get familiar with new words, but also helps to memorise the spellings in a better way.

The reader is given a set of words with jumbled alphabet and he/she needs to reconstruct the word to arrange the letters in the correct order to get the answer right. The jumbled word may consist of more than six letters. The reader is provided with clues. Each jumbled word has a clue related to it giving a hint to help the reader recognise the word.

Following is an example of a jumbled word with a clue:

U T F E A L B U I

Clue - An adjective used to appreciate a good looking person.

Answer – BEAUTIFUL

Exercise

Unjumble the words and write the right words with the given clues.

1) T G A I F U E

   Clue – A feeling of extreme physical or mental tiredness.

2) E R G O E T M U

   Clue – Nice, expensive and more sophisticated food.

3) G S O T N A I A L

   Clue – Affectionate feeling for the past.

4) I P T U O A

   Clue – An imaginary situation where the society is perfect and everyone is happy but it is practically impossible.

5) R A U V L O

   Clue – Great bravery, especially in a battle.

6) D M E I P D E T N I

   Clue – Person that makes others movement, development, or progress difficult.

7) M B T O C A

   Clue –Fighting that takes place in a war; another word for battle.

8) T C G I A G C I

   Clue –Something extremely large in size, amount, or degree.

9) I M A M E L D

Clue –A difficult situation in which one has to choose between two or more alternatives.

10) T E T P E P I A

Clue –The desire to eat.

11) R G E A E

Clue –A strong feeling to do or have something.

12) Y N R O I

Clue –Word explaining the situation which is odd or amusing because it involves a contrast.

13) L I A T V

Clue –Something that is necessary or very important.

14) I L I N T D E G

Clue –Someone who works hard in a careful and thorough way.

15) I A C U R C L

Clue –To describe something extremely important.

16) R I T U E T B

Clue –Something we say, do, or make to show our admiration and respect for someone.

17) D R N T A E

Clue –To describe someone who has extremely strong feelings about something or someone.

18) R N T V A B I

Clue –Someone or something that is full of life, energy, and enthusiasm.

19) N I N A C D R H E

Clue –A person or thing that makes it more difficult for you to do something.

20) L U N A R B E L V E

Clue –Someone who is weak and without protection, with the result that they are easily hurt physically or emotionally.

Unjumble the words and Write the right words with the given clues.

20) U F I F E S C

Clue: Enough to achieve a purpose or to fulfill a need.

21) M E T C N O E T L P A

Clue: For an idea or subject, you think about it carefully for a long time.

22) T I E O D N C R

Clue: A set of principles or beliefs, especially religious ones.

23) U L P R P E T A E

Clue: Feeling, state, or quality that never ends or changes.

24) L E X P R P E

Clue: Something that confuses or worries you because you do not understand it or because it causes you difficulty.

25) C R M E D O U

Clue: A behaviour that people consider to be correct, polite and respectable.

26) N D A O B N A

Clue: To leave a place, thing, or person permanently or for a long time, especially when you should not do so.

27) I N E T M O A N

Clue: To formally suggest a name as a candidate for a job or position.

28) L J A O V I

Clue: A person who is happy and behaves in a cheerful manner.

29) E O N C T L A E R

Clue: The quality of allowing other people to say and do as they like, even if you do not agree or approve of it.

30) R M A K B E

Clue: To start doing something new, difficult, or exciting.

31) O M C E M C E M

Clue: To start or begin something.

32) T E S O U P R

Clue: The position in which you stand or sit.

33) R C N O E N C

Clue: To worry about a situation or a person.

34) S O S E S P S

Clue: To have or own something.

35) R A I C D A T M

Clue: A change or event that happens suddenly and is very noticeable and surprising.

36) I R Y B L T E

Clue: The freedom to live your life in the way that you want, without interference.

37) S T N A D U O

Clue: Something by which you are very surprised.

38) U R E Q I V

Clue: Something shaking with very small movements.

39) X I E C T O

Clue: Something that is unusual and interesting, usually, because it comes from or is related to a distant country.

40) R G S E U L P

Clue: Spending a lot of money on something, usually on things that you do not need.

41) U I H L P B S

Clue: To print copies of books or magazines which are sent to shops to be sold.

42) M E C P T O R Y R A N O

Clue: Things which are modern and relate to the present time.

43) V H L I S A

Clue: Something that is very elaborate and impressive and a lot of money has been spent on it.

44) G A T E X E G A R E

Clue: To indicate that something is, for example, worse or more important than it really is.

45) E R D G U G

Clue: To have unfriendly feelings towards others because of something they did in the past.

46) L T N B A T A

Clue: Describing something bad that is done in an open or very obvious way.

47) I U M T M L U A T

Clue: A warning to someone that unless they act in a particular way, action will be taken against them.

48) E H E D W L E

Clue: People who try to persuade someone to do or give them what they want, for example by saying nice things that they don't mean.

49) O B P L A E R T

Clue: Machine or device designed to be easily carried or moved.

50) S L B T C E A O

Clue: An object that makes it difficult for you to go where you want to go, because it is in your way.

51) O S A U O C I T R

Clue: Emphasizing on something that is very bad in quality.

52) U E L P A L S I B

Clue: An explanation or statement that seems likely to be true or valid.

53) T O E D N E

Clue: Something that is a sign or indication of another thing.

54) Q Y E I U T

Clue: The quality of being fair and reasonable in a way that gives equal treatment to everyone.

55) I E T A M N P L U A

Clue: Disapprove of people because they skilfully force or persuade people to do what they want.

56) G E A T N E

Clue: One thing causing other thing to lose the effect or value that it had.

57) G A T I A N O I T

Clue: Someone in a state where he/she is worried or upset, and show this in his/her behaviour, movements or voice.

58) U E H L R D

Clue: A problem, difficulty, or a part of a process that may prevent you from achieving something.

59) B E M H L U

Clue: A person who is not proud and does not believe that they are better than other people.

ANTONYMS

The word, 'antonym' was coined in the 19th century by the philologists. The word, antonym comes from Greek, *anti (opposite)* and *onoma (name)*. This suggests that antonyms are words which have opposite meanings. The term, 'antonym' is synonymous with opposite. Antonyms tend to be *adverbs*, *adjectives* and *verbs* with relatively few nouns. Words opposite to each other may be similar in most other respects. One word may have more than one antonym.

Generally, our day to day English Vocabulary consists of antonyms and in order to improve one's vocabulary one needs to be familiar with them as they play an important role in helping to build a strong base of English.

For example:

An antonym for 'behave' would be 'misbehave'. Similarly, the opposite or antonym for 'agree' would be 'disagree'.

Inside – Outside

Balance – Imbalance

Dependent – Independent, etc.

Exercise

The following exercise provides the reader with a list of words given with two options each. The reader needs to select the right antonym out of the two choices to get the correct answer.

1) Overwrought

   a) agitated   b) calm

2) Contemptuous

   a) disdainful   b) respectful

3) Zeal

   a) apathy   b) fervour

4) Jagged

   a) smooth   b) spiky

5) Loyalty

   a) allegiance   b) treachery

6) Just

   a) unfair   b) fair

7) Guilty

   a) culpable   b) innocent

8) Rabble

   a) mob   b) nobility

9) Prone

a) vulnerable b) resistant

10) Lack

a) abundance b) deficiency

11) Adhere

a) detach b) separate

12) Alienate

a) harmonise b) patriotism

13) Adversity

a) prosperity b) accuracy

14) Acquit

a) convict b) innocent

15) Intentional

a) accidental b) deliberate

16) Optimist

a) pessimist b) opportunistic

17) attractive

a) repulsive b) compulsive

18) Abundant

a) immense b) scarce

19) Captivity

a) imprisonment b) liberty

20) Transparent

a) translucent b) opaque

Choose and tick the correct antonyms of the following words from the options given below the words.

1) Deterioration
   a) improvement   b) depletion
2) Erratic
   a) irregular   b) consistent
3) Factitious
   a) genuine   b) improper
4) Boisterous
   a) peaceful   b) noisy
5) Abstruse
   a) unsure   b) obvious
6) Hasten
   a) dawdle   b) industrious
7) Arrant
   a) array   b) partial
8) Capricious
   a) fickle   b) steadfast
9) Callow
   a) sophisticated   b) jejune
10) Craven
   a) brave   b) coward
11) Cynical
   a) selfish   b) trusting

12) Diabolical

a) seraphic b) merciful

13) Dilate

a) narrow b) broad

14) Emancipate

a) stifle b) enslave

15) Enmity

a) grudge b) affection

16) Destitute

a) impoverish b) affluent

17) Authentic

a) bogus b) genuine

18) Baleful

a) beneficent b) harmful

19) Anomaly

a) regularity b) irregularity

20) Flaunt

a) show off b) hide

21) Affirmative

a) positive b) negative

22) Compulsory

a) voluntary b) necessary

23) Elementary

a) basic b) advanced

24) Certainly

a) probably b) mostly

25) Exposure

a) secure b) shelter

26) Dictatorship

a) hierarchy b) democracy

27) Courageous

a) coward b) valour

28) Amateur

a) professional b) elementary

29) Feasible

a) sensible b) impractical

30) Eschew

a) welcome b) avoid

31) Dwindle

a) decrease b) increase

32) Divulge

a) secretive b) elusive

33) Eclectic

a) dogmatic b) clever

34) Dormant

a) lazy b) alert

35) Compatible

a) disagreement b) friendly

36) Benevolent

a) miserly b) calm

37) Adulterate

a) detach b) purify

38) Cogent

a) convincing b) unconvincing

39) Ensue

a) precede b) occur

40) Fantastic

a) unlikely b) realistic

SYNONYMS

The word, 'synonym' has been derived from the Greek word, *syn (with)* and *onoma (name)*. Synonyms are words or expressions with the same or nearly the same meanings. The words may be used as figurative or symbolic substitutes as they have identical meanings. They can be any parts of speech, such as nouns, verbs, adjectives, adverbs or prepositions. A word can have more than one synonym.

Synonyms are very useful. There are times when one avoids repeating the same words over and over again, and it becomes hard to think of an alternative word. A person well equipped with synonyms might not face these problems as the words come handy.

For example:

Synonyms for 'hardworking' are 'diligent', 'determined', 'industrious' and 'enterprising'. Similarly, synonyms for 'beautiful' are pretty, attractive, stunning and lovely and the synonyms for 'kind' are considerate, thoughtful, gracious, amiable, etc.

Exercise

The following exercise has three options out of which the reader has to opt for the most apt synonym for each of the given word.

1) Turbulent

   a) violent b) disturbing c) difficult

2) Hilarious

   a) amazing b) depressing c) humorous

3) Hypocrisy

   a) essential b) bureaucracy c) falseness

4) Significant

   a) infirm b) vital c) secure

5) Legitimate

   a) critical b) reliable c) authorised

6) Obsolete

   a) extinct b) disordered c) fragile

7) Embellish

   a) decorate b) instruct c) confront

8) Perpetrator

   a) victim b) culprit c) prisoner

9) Abandon

a) leave b) hate c) blame

10) Adept

a) follower b) believer c) skilled

11) Consent

a) accomplish b) agree c) fear

12) Vivacious

a) lively b) sorrow c) furious

13) Degrade

a) loathe b) ridiculous c) humiliate

14) Appalling

a) misgiving b) neutrality c) terrifying

15) Despotic

a) ease b) arbitrary c) suitable

16) Apprehend

a) seize b)worry c) adore

17) Elongated

a) flimsy b) malleable c) outstretched

18) Gallop

a) spring b) lengthy c) sprint

19) Obscure

a) frank b) peaceful c) hidden

20) Deceased

a) unwell b) misplace c) dead

Choose and tick the correct synonyms of the following words from the options given below the words.

1) Abandon

a) discard b) grant c) plentiful

2) Amenable

a) misfortunate b) favorable c) difficulty

3) Alleviate

a) rich b) mitigate c) vacate

4) Credulous

a) desire b) donation c) confident

5) Baffle

a) ignore b) confuse c) enlarge

6) Fervour

a) passion b) squalor c) nimble

7) Implicate

a) mammoth b) candid c) insinuate

8) Paramount

a) leading b) appease c) exclude

9) Tumult

a) convey b) commotion c) aggressive

10) Sanction

a) extent b) distinctive c) permit

11) Arraign

a) indict b) pacify c) inquire

12) Lucrative

a) misplaced b) insane c) profitable

13) Juvenile

a) estimate b) argot c) adolescent

14) Auspicious

a) clear b) lucky c) constraint

15) Negate

a) refute b) mandatory c) aspect

16) Persecute

a) harass b) effuse c) furor

17) Obstinate

a) atone b) deplore c) stubborn

18) Impromptu

a) subdue b) domesticate c) spontaneous

19) Partisan

a) dogmatic b) lethargic c) endure

20) Illustrious

a) perfection b) reflect c) eminent

21) Apparent

a) obvious b) strange c) unlikely

22) Applicable

a) imply b) relevant c) almost

23) Constitution

a) structure b) construct c) build

24) Fanatic

a) foolish b) optimistic c) enthusiastic

25) Deceptive

a) healing b) campaign c) misleading

26) Concord

a) elude b) harmony c) disturbing

27) Cherish

a) hate b) jealous c) love

28) Damp

a) moist b) drought c) rough

29) Omit

a) correct b) include c) exclude

30) Tame

a) balance b) temperature c) domesticate

31) Betray

a) confuse b) annoy c) deceive

32) Candid

a) daring b) allot c) truthful

33) Commemorate

a) natural b) desist c) celebrate

34) Eccentric

a) abnormal b) constant c) longing

35) Craving

a) denying b) believing c) longing

36) Dogma

a) earnest b) decline c) belief

37) Embezzle

a) foster b) radiate c) steal

38) Frivolous

a) angry b) trivial c) infirm

39) Haughty

a) arrogant b) coarse c) deceit

40) Manipulate

a) confine b) allude c) control

HOMOPHONES AND HOMONYMS

The words, 'homophones and homonyms' have originated from the Greek language. Both homophones and homonyms are vastly used in linguistics. *Homophones can be referred to as words that are pronounced the same as another word but have different meanings*. The words may or may not be spelt the same. The words which have different meanings but same pronunciations, and are spelt in the same way are known as *Homonyms*.

For example: Words, such as 'rose' (flower) and 'rose' (past tense of 'rise') are examples of homonyms and words like 'two' and 'to' are examples of homophones.

This topic can be divided into two sections, one consisting of exercise based on homophones and the other on homonyms. The first exercise is based on homophones, where the reader or the student is given two words to fill in the blanks in each sentence and the reader has to choose the correct answer for the correct blank.

Exercise

(HOMOPHONES)

1) The eagle's _________was on a lofty mountain peak in a bright and ________ location.

(airy, aerie)

2) _______and comfort are accorded to every patient by the nurses ________.

(aide, aid)

3) After we walk down the _______, I'll take you to an _______ of paradise for our honeymoon.

(isle, aisle)

4) The builder was sued for ________ of contract. The labourer dropped his shovel into the ________ of the excavation.

(breach, breech)

5) The ________ of the tree was bent by the wind as if to ________ in homage to nature.

(bow, bough)

6) The wooden _______ had several holes that had been _______ at different times.

(board, bored)

7) The robbers had a hidden _______ of diamonds, jewellery and _______.

(cash, cashe)

8) The supervisor wrote a schedule on the ________ to indicate the days that the operator should oil the _________.

(calender, calendar)

9) What _______ to the beauty of subtractive wood sculpting, is the careful use of the _______.

(adds, adz)

10) One should ________ a will or reveal the contents of ________ a death that may exclude an unnamed _________.

(ere, heir, air)

11) After the ________ had laboured to complete the poetry, the authorities ________ it from the recital.

(bard, barred)

12) The church __________ attracted many strangers, some of them dressed and acted in __________ ways.

(bizarre, bazaar)

13) Her loving ________ brought a ________ for her hair.

(beau, bow)

14) The _________ winds through the valley made all the doors of the house _________.

(creek, creak)

Fill in the blanks with the correct homophones from the options given within the brackets.

1) The __________ played such cacophonous music throughout the performance that it was __________ from further auditions.

(banned, band)

2) The lower __________ of a railroad sleeper car was the only available place for her to give __________ to the baby.

(berth, birth)

3) With confused expressions, the book sales persons furrowed their _________ when the student proceeded to ___________through every book in the store.

(brows, browse)

4) Have you read the story about the tortoise and the _________________________?

(hair, hare)

5) The ____________ flew overhead and screeched ___________!

(awk, auk)

6) When the _____________ bounced over the fence and out of reach, the child began to _____________ and sob.

(bawl, ball)

7) He had to ____________ the drums for four hours before he was entitled to a dinner which included an entree, a _____________salad and a beverage.

(beat, beet)

8) One may find a _________ tree in a nudist colony where humans are _________; in a circus, clothes are put on animals such as dog, monkey and ___________.

(bare, bair, bear)

9) She had _________fuelling the fire with the cord of oak that she had found in the wood ______________.

(bin, been)

10) A ________ of hay was dropped from the airplane for the hungry cattle, the ranchers then began to __________ out one by one.

(bale, bail)

11) It is hard to imagine that the ___________of Manhattan had carts drawn by __________on the streets where subways now ____________ below.

(burrow, burro, borough)

12) The _________ weevil came out of the cotton field, crawled around the ___________ of the large oak and rested on our picnic sugar _________.

(bowl, boll, bole)

13) The jockey held the horse's _____________ lightly.

(rein, reign)

14) The engine failed so they _____________ the boat back home.

(rode, rowed)

15) Roosters are a favourite weather _________ design.

(vein, vane)

Exercise

(HOMONYMS)

This one is a guessing exercise based on homonyms. The given sentences are clues to the oneword answers which have the same pronunciations and spellings but different meanings. The word in each case should be appropriate to make sense for both the sentences as they are in different contexts.

1) Opposite for hit/Mr., Mrs., __________.
2) A musical instrument you blow/two of these can be found on a bull's head.
3) A place with lots of games and rides/to treat people without favouritism.
4) Opposite of right/past tense of leave.
5) Child / baby goat/to trick someone.
6) You can wear these to help you see better/you can serve drinks in them.
7) The substance used to make tyres/something used to erase pencil.
8) A container/type of plant/to fight with fists.
9) Not moving/continuing to do something.
10) To look after something/your brain.

11) You hit one with a hammer/there is one on the end of every finger.

12) To fire a gun/a new growth on a plant.

13) A boy's name/a teacher can ________ your work.

14) Opposite of hot/if you catch one you sneeze.

15) A month/could

16) You have to pay this for doing wrong/the weather can be _____(sunny)

17) A place where someone is buried/serious __________

18) You can _______ your name/you can make a_______ with your hand

19) You can kick, throw, or catch this/Cindrella went to one.

20) You strike this to get a flame/you can have a football __________.

This one is a guessing exercise based on homonyms. The given sentences are clues to the one-word answers which have same pronunciations and spellings, but different meanings. The word in each case should be appropriate to make sense for both the sentences as they are in different contexts.

1) This tells you how much to pay/ a beak of a bird / boy's name.
2) Jump often using a rope / miss something.
3) To create a picture on paper / a result of a match where neither team wins.
4) A flower / found in your eye.
5) Look at this / to see what the time is.
6) Practice for a match / travel on the rails.
7) Press down hard with you foot / to stick this on the envelope.
8) A learner / in the middle of an eye.
9) A place where students learn / a group of fish.
10) A keen supporter / to cool you down.
11) Move your hand / as the water comes in.
12) Less heavy / way to start a fire.
13) Shake with fear / holding the arrows.
14) Smooth / not odd numbers.
15) A season / to go boing!
16) A tree / in the middle of your hand.

PREFIX AND SUFFIX

Prefixes and Suffixes are widely used in order to form new words or to alter the meanings of the words by adding a group of letters before or after each word. The group of letters added in front of the word is known as *prefix* and the group of letters added at the end of the word is known as *suffix*.

The exercise below will target on readers' skills of analysing each word. The reader has been provided with a word and its meaning, and one has to add a prefix or a suffix to the word in order to alter the meaning.

For example:

He was acting in a very ____________________ way. (child)

Answer-childish

Exercise

1) He was sitting __________________ in his seat on the train. (comfort)
2) Some of the shanty towns are dreadfully __________________. (crowd)
3) This word is very difficult to spell, and even worse, it's __________________. (pronounce)
4) You need to be a highly trained __________________ to understand this report. (economy)
5) There were only a __________________ of people at the match. (hand)
6) He wants to be a __________________ when he grows up. (mathematics)
7) They had to __________________ the lion before they could catch it. (tranquil)
8) You need a ________________ of motivation, organisation and revision to learn English. (combine)
9) His __________________ has been expected for the last half an hour. (arrive)
10) She had no __________________ of going to see him. (intend)

11) Failing her driving test was a great __________________ to her. (appoint)

12) He decided to study __________________ at university. (journal)

13) With the real plan, the rate of __________________ in Brazil has fallen. (inflate)

14) The party was __________________ , everything went wrong. (disaster)

15) The event was totally __________________ . It was terrible. (organised)

16) He was __________________ . He wouldn't change his mind. (compromise)

17) He spent half an hour __________________ himself with the building. (familiar)

18) She looked at her __________________ in the mirror. (reflect)

19) The team that he supported were able to win the__________________ . (champion)

20) He didn't pass his exam. He was __________________ for the second time. (succeed)

The exercise below will target on the readers' skills of analysing each word. The reader has been provided with a word and its meaning and one has to add a prefix or a suffix to the word in order to alter the meaning.

1) Tricia was _______________________ to visit her friend because she had a lot of homework to do. (able)
2) Christian ___________________________ his jacket when he came inside the house. (buttoned)
3) Please help you mother ______________________the groceries from the car. (load)
4) This broken toy is a ___________________________ piece of junk.(worth)
5) He needed to _________________ the temperature. (regular)
6) I told him my plan but he wasn't very_________________ . (receive)
7) The film was _________________ good. (surprise)
8) It really isn't mine. I think that you are_________________ . (take)
9) Have you seen that new _________________ ? He's very funny. (comedy)
10) The company has over 500 _________________ . (employ)
11) The road was too narrow, so they had to _________________ it. (wide)
12) He was _________________ . He wouldn't change his mind. (compromise)

13) He's lost his book again. I don't know where he has ___________________ it this time. (place)

14) You shouldn't have done that! It was very ___________________ of you. (think)

15) Dad is _____________________ bacon for breakfast. (fry)

16) Amy's brother has not come home yet and she is _____________________ about him. (worry)

17) Grady likes to draw and paint pictures. He is an _____________________________. (art)

18) Ms. Cadbury arranges flowers for a living. She is a ______________________. (flower)

19) Will _________________________ his parents. (obey)

20) Mrs. Wu said she does not want ______ _________ homework handed in. (finish)

IDIOMS, PROVERBS & PHRASES

A combination of words which have figurative meanings are called *idioms or phrases*. These are expressions which are often metaphorical and separate from the literal meaning or definition of words. There are numerous idioms and phrases used in our everyday conversations making the language more colourful.

For example:

a) *Piece of cake*:
something which is very easy.

b) *Dress to kill*:
to wear one's finest clothes.

c) *Adding fuel to the fire*:
to make a bad situation even worse.

Exercise

(IDIOMS)

The first exercise below is based on idioms. There will be various idioms from which the reader has to choose the correct idiom to fill in each of the blanks in the following sentences.

i. Barking up the wrong tree
ii. Out of the blue
iii. Fly by the seat of her pants
iv. Like a third wheel
v. Get his act together
vi. Off his rocker
vii. Butterflies in my stomach
viii. Like the pot calling the kettle black
ix. Get a word in edgewise
x. Off in the clouds
xi. Some song and dance
xii. Hit the roof
xiii. Throw the book at him
xiv. Chickens with their heads cut off
xv. Blow off some steam
xvi. Burn the midnight oil

xvii. In the red

xviii. Searching for a needle in the haystack

xix. Burning the candle at both ends

xx. Run circles around

Choose the correct idiom or phrase for each of the following sentences:

1) If he doesn't______________, he'll be forced to leave the school.

2) My boss will ______________if those papers are not found.

3) At dinner with my roommate and his girlfriend, I felt__________.

4) He gave us ______________about why the work wasn't finished.

5) This is his third offense and the police should ________________.

6) Our offense was able to ________________around their defense.

7) Before giving my speech in front of the whole class, I had ________________.

8) When the lunchroom is busy, the cafeteria workers run around ____________________________.

9) After giving that crazy lecture that made no sense, we thought our teacher was________________.

10) If you think that I stole your jacket, you're______________.

11) Physical exercise is a good way to________________.

12) Instead of__________________, you need to cut back on some of your activities and commitments.

13) During the week of final exams, many students will ________________.

14) Finding a contact lens on a crowded dance floor is like ______________________________.

15) Dad accusing you of eating too much is like the _______ __________________________.

16) One day, ________________, I got a call from a friend I hadn't heard from in years.

17) How does he pay the bills when his business is always_______________?

18) He seldom pays attention in class and it seems that his head is ____________________.

19) Finding the student unprepared for class, the teacher had to ____________________.

20) He didn't use complete sentences until he was 4 years old, but then no one could ____________________________.

This exercise is based on idioms. There are given be various idioms from which the reader has to choose the correct idiom for each of the sentences given below. One has been done for you.

a) rounded off
b) flew off
c) close call
d) telling tales
e) as true as steel
f) hang its head
g) have itchy feet
h) brushed away
i) Thanks a bunch
j) through the floor
k) coming out of his ears
l) at death's door
m) top of the hour
n) nuts and bolts
o) gnashed his teeth
p) in the dark
q) waiting to catch the next wave.
r) point of view
s) dead letter
t) steamed out

1) Apparently it was a *close call*, but after a long debate the jury convicted her.
2) He has no purpose in life. He sits around strumming his guitar and waiting to catch the next wave.
3) Every class in my school starts at the top of the hour.
4) We rounded off the meal with a sinful dessert.
5) She brushed away the crumbs from the table.
6) Law school teaches wonderful theory but it doesn't teach the nuts and bolts of actually practising law.
7) Thanks a bunch for your help.
8) Through all my troubles, my husband has been as true as steel.
9) I had half a mind to tell my boss about him but I didn't want her to think I was telling tales.
10) Why've you got all these travel brochures? Do you have itchy feet?
11) Dave flew off with his brother because they had to meet a train.
12) He literally was at death's door when a liver became available for transplant.
13) House prices have gone through the floor this year.
14) It shuddered a couple of times and steamed out.
15) His point about the need for education reform is a dead letter.
16) From my point of view, all this talk is a waste of time.
17) Bill clenched his fists and gnashed his teeth in anger.
18) I'm in the dark about who is in charge around here.
19) He's going to have money coming out of his ears if this deal comes off.
20) Though our team lost, it played well and had no need to hang its head.

Exercise

(PHRASES)

A group of words within a sentence or a clause is referred to as *phrases.* The phrase functions as a unit and includes a head which determines the type or nature of the phrase.

For example:

When this is all over, your father might be ***going away*** for a little while.

Here ***going away*** is the phrase telling the nature of the sentence i.e., phrasal verb.

Fill in the blanks using the appropriate phrase from the options given below the sentences in each case:

1) You must ______________ and make plans for the future.

   a) Look on b) Look up

   c) Look ahead d) Look back

2) There were so many panes of glass broken that the windows couldn't ______________ the rain.

   a) keep on b) keep up

   c) keep out d) keep back

3) Children have a natural inclination to look ______________ to their parents.

a) Forward to b) Up to

c) Out on d) Back to

4) He looks ______________ me because I spend my holidays in *India* instead of going abroad.

a) Down at b) Down on

c) Out of d) Back on

5) The crowd ____________ while the police surrounded the house.

a) Looked on b) Looked up

c) Looked out d) Looked at

6) I had to wait for permission from the Town Council before I could __________________ with my plans.

a) Go round b) Go up

c) Go on d) Go back

7) He ____________ his mother; he has blue eyes and fair hair.

a) Takes out b) Takes up

c) Takes on d) Takes after

8) Don't ____________with the idea that Scotsmen are mean. They just don't like wasting money.

a) Run out b) Run away

c) Run on d) Run off

9) I __________ to an old school friend in the tube today.

a) Ran in b) Ran up

c) Ran on d) Ran off

10) I _______ Tom in chess and beat him.

a) Took out b) Took up

c) Took on d) Took off

11) As a parent, you should _______________ such small mistakes from the kids.

a) Allow into b) Allow for

c) Allow with d) Make allowances

12) The principal became furious on hearing the news of the students' unrest but eventually _____________.

a) calmed into b) calmed down

c) calmed over d) calmed up

13) For the sake of his health, Siddhu decided to __________ smoking.

a) Give through b) Give along

c) Give up d) Give for

14) The teacher requested the class representative to ____________ the answer sheets to all the students.

a) Hand at b) Hand on

c) Hand back d) Hand out

15) Tina eagerly ___________ the day her exams would get over and she would be back to partying with her friends.

a) Looked forward to b) Looked after

c) Looked up to d) Looked down on

16) It took the firemen a long time to __________ the blazing fire.

a) Put off	b) Put out

c) Put on	d) Put up

17) I wanted to ______________ the dress before buying it, in order to check if it was the right size for me.

a) Rely on	b) Take on

c) Look on	d) Try on

18) Aisha ___________ her mother to a great degree.

a) Takes off	b) Took out

c) Takes on	d) Takes after

19) The policeman was quick to ____________ the number of the speeding car.

a) Back down	b) Calm down

c) Note down	d) Let down

20) After the movie got over, she decided to ______________ with her friends till the evening.

a) Hang out	b) Hang up

c) Hurry up	d) Iron out

Fill in the blanks using the appropriate phrases from the options given below the sentences in each case:

1) She ____________ some old love letters.

   a) came by　　b) came across

   c) came out　　d) came around

2) I ______________ but nobody has seen my wallet.

   a) asked about　　b) asked in

   c) asked out　　d) asked around

3) Your purchases ______________ to $205.32.

   a) add up　　b) add in

   c) add out　　d) add off

4) You'll have to ______________ your car so that I can get out.

   a) back behind　　b) back in

   c) back around　　d) back up

5) The racing car ______________ after it crashed into the fence.

   a) blew off　　b) blew into

   c) blew up　　d) blew by

6) Our car ________________ at the side of the highway in the snowstorm.

   a) broke up　　b) broke down

   c) broke into　　d) broke out

7) Somebody ________________ last night and stole our stereo.

   a) broke in　　b) broke inside

   c) broke into　　d) broke out

8) The firemen had to ______________ the room to rescue the children.

a) break in b) break inside

c) break into d) break out

9) My mother ________________ of the room when my father brings up sports.

a) walks off b) walks outside

c) walks up d) walks out

10) We _______________ but we weren't able to find the car part we needed.

a) called out b) called off

c) called around d) called up

11) You are still mad. You need to ___________ before you drive the car.

a) calm down b) calm off

c) calm into d) calm in

12) You'll have to run faster than that if you want to __________ with Marty.

a) catch in b) catch up

c) catch after d) catch

13) You have to ____________ of the hotel before 11:00 AM.

a) check off b) check outside

c) check in d) check out

14) If everyone _____________ we can get the kitchen painted by noon.

a) chips together
b) chips after
c) chips in
d) chips for

15) The top and bottom _______________ if you pull hard enough.

a) come apart
b) come out
c) come together
d) come off

16) I am ______________ you to make dinner while I am out.

a) counting in
b) counting into
b) counting on
d) counting onto

17) My doctor wants me to ____________ on sweets and fatty foods.

a) cut back
b) cut down
c) cut out
d) cut off

18) The doctors _____________ his leg because it was severely injured.

a) cut back
b) cut down
c) cut out
d) cut off

19) I _______________ of Science because it was too difficult.

a) dropped into
b) dropped off
c) dropped out
d) dropped down

20) We _____________ renting a movie instead of going to the theatre.

a) ended up
b) ended onto
c) ended into
d) ended out

21) The picture that you _____________ last night fell down this morning.

a) hung onto
b) hung in
c) hung up
d) hung out

22) Jason always _____________ with cheating in his maths tests.

a) gets around
b) gets off
c) gets ahead
d) gets away

23) Let's _______________-for a BBQ this weekend.

a) get away
b) get together
c) get around
d) get off

24) We are _______________-the best soccer team in the city tonight.

a) going against
b) going ahead
c) going opposite
d) going for

25) We are _____________our trip until January because of the hurricane.

a) putting out
b) putting off
c) putting on
d) putting ahead

26) It's a fancy restaurant so we have to _______________.

a) dress in
b) dress around
c) dress over
d) dress up

27) The money must have ______________ of my pocket.

a) fallen off b) fallen out

c) fallen over d) fallen above

28) My maths homework was too difficult so I__________-.

a) gave in b) gave off

c) gave up d) gave out

29) My roses ____________ this summer.

a) grew back b) grew out

c) grew over d) grew on

30) ______________ while I grab my coat and shoes!

a) hang on b) hang up

c) hang off d) hang out

31) Jamie ______________ his tears at his grandfather's funeral.

a) held below b) held before

c) held on d) held back

32) I have to ________________ my sick grandmother.

a) look before b) look after

c) look over d) look on

33) I ________________ the twins' names again!

a) mixed in b) mixed over

c) mixed up d) mixed on

34) We ______________ of shampoo so I had to wash my hair with soap.

a) ran over b) ran out

c) ran off d) ran in

35) When I ______________ on my youth, I wish I had studied harder.

a) think of b) think before

c) think back d) think after

Exercise

(PROVERBS)

Proverbs, on the other hand are short and pithy sayings which express wisdom or advice and some traditionally held truth. These statements are metaphorical in nature and are transmitted from generation to generation.

For example:

a) Where there's a will there's a way:

when a person really wants to do something, he will find a way of doing it no matter what.

b) All that glitters is not gold:

Do not be deceived by things or offers that appear to be attractive.

The reader has to find the right proverb from the given choices in each case and match them with their meanings given below:

1) Uneasy lies the head that wears the crown.
2) Wake not a sleeping lion.
3) Waste not, want not.
4) Where ignorance is bliss, it is folly to be wise.
5) The wish is the father to the thought.

6) Nothing ventured, nothing gained.
7) Every ass likes to hear himself bray.
8) The apple doesn't fall far from the tree.
9) Still waters run deep.
10) The die is cast.
11) The road to hell is paved with good intentions.
12) Time and tide wait for no man.
13) Two wrongs don't make a right.
14) Virtue is its own reward.
15) The end justifies the means.

Meanings:

i. Children resemble their parents.
ii. If one is careful with things especially money, one will not lack them when needed.
iii. It is wrong to harm someone because they have harmed you.
iv. You should not expect praise for acting in a correct or moral way.
v. Without risks, there are no rewards.
vi. Wrong or unfair methods may be used if the result of the action is good.
vii. A quiet person can have much knowledge or wisdom.
viii. One must not miss opportunities by delaying action.
ix. With greatness and power comes a lot of responsibilities.
x. It is not enough to intend to do something , you must actually do it.
xi. Foolish people talk a lot.

xii. It is wise not to disturb things at times lest you invite trouble.

xiii. The decision has been made and its impossible to change.

xiv. You think that something is true because you want it to be so.

xv. It is better to be unaware of something that will bring unhappiness.

The reader has to find the right proverb from the given choices in each case and match them with their meanings given below:

1) absence makes the heart grow fonder
2) all fish are not caught with flies
3) all cats are gray in the dark
4) all roads lead to Rome
5) an army marches on its stomach
6) blood is thicker than water
7) care is no cure
8) don't wash your dirty linen in public
9) good wine needs no bush
10) hunger drives the wolf out of the wood
11) hurry no man's cattle
12) justice is blind
13) love is free
14) man is the measure of all things
15) peace makes plenty
16) seize the day
17) you can't unscramble eggs
18) when in doubt, do nothing
19) to each his own
20) whose bread I eat, his song I sing

Meanings

i. People have no distinguishing features, and their appearances become unimportant, in the dark.
ii. Peace brings prosperity.
iii. People tend to fall in love regardless of the suitability of the match or other obstacles.

iv. Worrying about something does nothing to put it right.
v. Justice must be dispensed with objectivity and without regard to irrelevant details or circumstances.
vi. Your affection for those close to you—family and friends—increases when you are parted from them.
vii. In some circumstances different methods must be employed to achieve a desired end.
viii. There are many different ways to achieve the same result, or to come to the same conclusion.
ix. If you are unsure what to do, it is best to do nothing at all.
x. Human beings are capable of rising to any challenge.
xi. Everybody has his or her own tastes and idiosyncrasies.
xii. Live for the present, and take full advantage of every moment.
xiii. You must eat well if you want to work effectively or achieve great things.
xiv. Do not try to make others hurry or rush because you are impatient.
xv. Bonds of loyalty and affection between members of the same family are much stronger than any other relationship.
xvi. People in dire need are forced to do things that would be unwise or undesirable in other circumstances.
xvii. A good product does not need advertising.
xviii. Do not discuss private disputes or family scandals in public.
xix. People show loyalty to, or comply with the demands of, those who employ, pay, or feed them.
xx. Damage cannot be undone, and changes cannot be reversed.

ACRONYMS

An an acronym or abbreviation is formed by taking the initial letters or group of letters taken from a word or series of words, that is itself pronounced as a word.

Such as ROM – Read Only Memory

Exercise

Below are a few commonly used acronyms and the reader has to write the full form against each of them.

1) RADAR
2) NAAFI
3) NASA
4) LASER
5) SCUBA
6) UNESCO
7) AIDS
8) SAT
9) PIN
10) RAM

Given below are a few commonly used acronyms and the reader has to write the full form against each of them.

1) Maser
2) Internet
3) Sonar
4) SWAT
5) BASIC
6) BIOS
7) AHEAD
8) STEPS
9) UNICEF
10) UNESCO

Answers

WORD SEARCH

1)

+AY++++++DY++

+F+D++++O+N++

+F++R++M++O++

+E+++AI+T+M++

+C+++NPO++R++

+T++A+IO++A++

+I+T+R++E+H++

+OE+T++++J+++

+N+AMUSING+++

++P++++++++++

++++HSINIMID+

+++++++++++++

++++++++++++++

2)

FCHASE++++++B

L++++++E++++R

A+++++M+E+++U

M+++NOISULLIT

B+++TYT+++++R

O + + I + A S + + + + + + E
Y + P + B + + A + + + + + P
A E + L + + + + + T + + + +
N + I + + + + + + + N + + +
T S + + + + + + + + + A + +
H + + + + + + + + + + + F +
+ + + + + + + + + + + + + + +
+ + + + + + + + + + + + + + +

3)

+ R + + + + + + + + + H + +
+ + E + + + + + + + + S + +
+ + + V + + + + + + + I + +
E Z I N I T U R C S N + +
T + + + + V + + + Y E + +
+ E + + + + E + F + L + +
F + R + + + + + I + + P + +
I + + P + + L + + + E + +
C + + + R P + + + + R + +
K + + + M E P I V O T A L
L + + E + + T + + + + + + +
E + X + + + + + N + + + + +
+ E + + + + + + + I + + + +

4)

H + E + + + + + + + I + + E
+ A + N + + + + + L N + + R
+ + L + I + + U + G + + O
+ + + L + L C + + E + + D

+ + + + U R C L + N + + A
+ + + + A C I N + I + + +
+ + + T + P I + I O + + +
+ + I + U + + N + U + + +
+ V + P + + + + A S + + +
E D A U S R E P + T + + +
+ + + + + + + + + + I + +
+ + + + + + + + + + + O +
+ + + + + + + + + + + N +

5)

+ D + + R + + + + + + + +
+ E + + + A + + + + S + A
+ L + + + T T + + U + S +
+ I + + + N + I O + S + +
+ C + + + E + I O A + + +
+ A + + + M C + U N + + +
+ T + + + A + L + + A + +
+ E + + U R T + + + + L +
+ + + Q T E N D E N C Y +
+ + O + + P + + + + + + +
+ L + + + M + + + + + + +
+ + + + + E + + + + + + +
+ + + + + T E G A G N E +

6)

+ + + + + + + + + A L + +
+ + + + + + + + L + A + +

+ + + + E + + L + + U E +

+ + + + + T E + + + T + +

C I T A M G A R P U R + +

+ + + + A + + U C + I + +

I + + T + + + E Q + V + +

+ M I + + + X + + E + + +

+ O P + + E + + + + D + +

N + + O + B A F F L E A +

+ + + + S + + + + + + + +

+ + + + + E + + + + + + +

+ + + + + + + + + + + + + +

7)

+ N + + + + + + E + E + +

+ O + + + + + X + V + + +

+ I + + + + P + I + + + +

+ T + + + L + S + + + + +

+ A + M O D N A R + + + P

+ V S R + E + + + + + + R

+ O E A F + + + + + + + E

+ N + F B + + + + + + + V

+ N O B N O X I O U S + E

+ I + + + + T + + + + + N

+ + + + + + + A + + + + T

+ + + + + + + + G + + + +

+ + + + + + + + + + E + + +

8)

Y + C + + + + + + + H M R +
+ R + O + + + + S + U E +
+ + A + N + + I + + L V +
+ + + R + C N + + + U E +
+ + + + O E I + + + C N +
+ + + + L P + S + + I G +
+ + + P + + M + E + R E +
+ + E + + + + E + + R + +
+ R + + + + + F T + U + +
E N G R A V E + + N C + +
+ + + + + T + + + + O + +
+ + + + C + + + + + + C +
+ + + H + + + + + + + + +

9)

+ E + + + + + + + + + E A
+ + T + + + + + + + + S B
+ + + A R E T I R E + N A
+ + + + I + + + + + + E T
+ + + + + L + L + + + C E
T N E M R I A P M I + I +
+ + I + + U + T + + + L +
+ + + M T + + + E + + + +
+ + + C P + + + + R + + +
+ + A + + A + + + + + + +
+ F + + + + C + + + + + +

+ + + + + + + + T + + + + +
+ + + + + + + + + + + + + + +

10)

+ + + + + + + + + + T + + +
S + + N + + + + + + C + + +
+ U + A + + H + + I + + +
+ + O G + S + + + R + + +
S U O M I N A N U T + + +
+ + + D A O + + + S + + +
+ + D + + F B + + E + + +
+ A + + + + N S + R + + +
F + + + + + + + I C + + + +
+ + P O P U L A R E + + +
+ + + + + + + + + + + N + +
+ + + + + + + + + + + + E +
+ + + + + + + + + + + + + + +

11)

+ + + + + + I + S + + + + +
+ + + + A C + U + + + + + +
C + + B + O + O T + + + + +
+ O Y + + N + E + L + + +
+ S N + + I + N + + U + +
S + + S + C + E + + + C +
+ + + + O + + G + + + + + +
+ + + + + L + O + + + + + +
+ + + + + + + E M + + + + + +

+ + + + + + + + O C I P E +

+ + + + + + + + H + + + + + +

S A C R I F I C E + + + +

+ + + + + + + + + + + + + +

12)

N + D + + + + + + + A + R R

+ O + A + + + + S + E C E

+ + I + N + + T + T + H D

+ + + T + G O + T + + A N

+ + + + U N E U + + + L U

+ + + + I A + R + + + L L

+ + + S + + C + O + + E B

+ + H + + + + + + U + N +

E R I P S N I + + + S G +

+ + + + + + + + + + + + E +

+ + + + + + + + + + + + + +

+ + + + + + + + + + + + + +

+ + + + + + + + + + + + + +

13)

+ + T + + + + + H + E H +

+ + + E + + + + E U + T +

+ + + + G + + + T + + U +

+ + + + + D + H E + + O +

C I O R E H A M R + + Y +

T O U G H N A G O + + + +

+ + + + A L + + G + + + +

+ + + S B + + + E + + + +
+ + I + + + + + N + + + +
+ A + + + + + + E + + + +
+ + + + + + + + O + + + +
+ + + + + + + + U + + + +
+ + + + + + + + S + + + +

14)

+ + + + + + + + + + + + +
+ + + + + + + + + + + O +
A + + + + + + + + + O Y +
+ L + + + + + + + B + N +
C O L L A B O R A T E O +
+ + + E + + + T C + M M +
+ + + + G + + E + + B E +
+ + + + + A R + + + A G +
+ + + + + E T + + + R E +
+ + + + M + + I + + R H +
+ + + O + + + + O + A + +
+ + N + + + + + + N S + +
+ Y N O I S A C C O S + +

15)

+ + + N + + + + + + R + E
+ + + + O + + + + E + + B
+ + + T + I + + G + E + I
+ + + E + + T E + R + + R
+ + + M + + N A U + + + C

+ + + P + E + T V + + + S
+ + + T R + L + + L + + B
+ + + A + U + + + + A + U
+ + T T C + + + + + + S S
+ E + I E R U T N E V D A
+ + + O + + A C H I E V E
+ + + N + + + + + + + + +
+ + + + + + + + + + + + +

16)

+ + + + + + + + + P + H N
D N E F F O + + + O U + I
E + + + C + + + + R + + A
+ V + + + O + + D T + + V
+ + E + + + M L + I + + +
+ + + I + + E P + O + + +
+ + + + R + + + O N + + +
+ + + + + G + + + U + + +
+ + + + + + + + + + N + +
O P P O R T U N I T Y D +
+ + + + + + + + + + + + +
+ + + + + + + + + + + + +
+ + + + + + + + + + + + +

17)

+ + + + + + W + + + + + +
+ + + + + + + O + + + + +
L A V O R P P A L E + + +

Y + + + + + + B S L + + +
T E X T E N T U A + A + +
E + + + + + F + + F + H +
I + + + + F + + + + F + S
R + + + I T + + + + + L +
A + + D + R + + + + + + E
V + + + + E + + + + + + +
+ + + + + N + + + + + + +
+ + + + + D + + + + + + +
+ + + + + + + + + + + + +

18)

E + + T + + + + E + R + +
C V + + I + + T + A + + +
O + A + + M A + D + + + +
N + + L + N D I + + + + +
F + + + U + C A + + + + +
E + + T M A N D A T O R Y
S + R + L + T + + + + + +
S O + + + + + E + + + + +
F + + + + + + + + + + + +
+ Y F I C A P + + + + + +
+ + + + + + + + + + + + +
+ + + + + + + + + + + + +
+ + + + + + + + + + + + +

19)

+ + + + + + + E C + + + +

+ P + + + + T + I + + + +

+ + R + + A + + T E + + +

+ + + E T + + + E N + + +

+ + + I D + + + H H + + +

+ + D + + I + + T A + + +

+ E + + + + C + A N + + P

M W O R R O S T P C + O +

A P P R A I S E A E N + +

+ + + + + + + + + D + + +

+ + + + + + + + E + + + +

+ + + + + + + R + + + + +

+ + + + + + + + + + + + +

20)

+ + G + + + E + + D D + +

+ + + N + L + + I + N + +

+ + + + I + + S + + U + +

+ + + R + N D + + + O + +

+ + E + + A R + + + F + +

+ T + + I + + A + + N + +

S + + N + + B + E + O + +

+ + F + + + + O + Y C + +

+ U O P P O S E A + + + +

L + + + + + + + + S + + +

+ + + + + + + + + + T + +

G N I L L A P P A + + + +

JUMBLED WORDS

1) Fatigue
2) Gourmet
3) Nostalgia
4) Utopia
5) Valour
6) Impediment
7) Combat
8) Gigantic
9) Dilemma
10) Appetite
11) Eager
12) Irony
13) Vital
14) Diligent
15) Crucial
16) Tribute
17) Ardent
18) Vibrant
19) Hindrance
20) Vulnerable

---

1) Suffice
2) Contemplate
3) Doctrine
4) Perpetual
5) Perplex
6) Decorum
7) Abandon
8) Nominate
9) Jovial
10) Tolerance
11) Embark
12) Commence
13) Posture
14) Concern
15) Possess
16) Dramatic
17) Liberty
18) Astound

19) Quiver
20) Exotic
21) Splurge
22) Publish
23) Contemporary
24) Lavish
25) Exaggerate
26) Grudge
27) Blatant
28) Ultimatum
29) Wheedle
30) Portable
31) Obstacle
32) Atrocious
33) Plausible
34) Denote
35) Equity
36) Manipulate
37) Negate
38) Agitation
39) Hurdle
40) Humble

ANTONYMS

1) Calm
2) Respectful
3) Apathy
4) Smooth
5) Treachery
6) Unfair
7) Innocent
8) Nobility
9) Resistant
10) Abundance
11) Detach
12) Harmonise
13) Prosperity
14) Convict
15) Accidental
16) Pessimist
17) Repulsive
18) Scarce
19) Liberty
20) Opaque

---

1) Improvement
2) Consistent
3) Genuine
4) Peaceful
5) Obvious
6) Dawdle
7) Partial
8) Steadfast
9) Sophisticated
10) Brave
11) Trusting
12) Seraphic
13) Narrow
14) Enslave
15) Affection
16) Affluent
17) Bogus
18) Beneficent
19) Regularity
20) Hide

21) Negative
22) Voluntary
23) Advanced
24) Probably
25) Shelter
26) Democracy
27) Coward
28) Professional
29) Impractical
30) Avoid
31) Increase
32) Secretive
33) Dogmatic
34) Alert
35) Disagreement
36) Miserly
37) Purify
38) Unconvincing
39) Precede
40) Realistic

SYNONYMS

1) Violent
2) Humorous
3) Falseness
4) Vital
5) Authorized
6) Extinct
7) Decorate
8) Culprit
9) Leave
10) Skilled
11) Agree
12) Lively
13) Humiliate
14) Terrifying
15) Arbitrary
16) Seize
17) Outstretched
18) Sprint
19) Hidden
20) Dead

---

1) Discard
2) Favorable
3) Mitigate
4) Confident
5) Confuse
6) Passion
7) Insinuate
8) Leading
9) Commotion
10) Permit
11) Indict
12) Profitable
13) Adolescent
14) Lucky
15) Refute
16) Harass
17) Stubborn
18) Spontaneous
19) Dogmatic
20) Eminent

21) Obvious
22) Relevant
23) Structure
24) Enthusiast
25) Misleading
26) Harmony
27) Love
28) Moist
29) Exclude
30) Domesticate
31) Deceive
32) Truthful
33) Celebrate
34) Abnormal
35) Longing
36) Belief
37) Steal
38) Trivial
39) Arrogant
40) Control

HOMOPHONES

1) Aerie, airy
2) Aid, aide
3) Aisle, isle
4) Breach, breech
5) Bough, bow
6) Board, bored
7) Cahse, cash
8) Calendar, calendar
9) Adds, adz
10) Air, ere, heir
11) Bard, barred
12) Bazaar, bizarre
13) Beau, bow
14) Creek, creak
15) Principal, principle

---

1) Band, banned
2) Berth, birth
3) Brows, browse
4) Hare
5) Auk, awk
6) Ball, bawl
7) Beat, beet
8) Bair, bare, bear
9) Been, bin
10) Bale, bail
11) Borough,burro, burrow
12) Boll, bole, bowl
13) Rein
14) Rowed
15) Vane

HOMONYMS

1) Miss
2) Horn
3) Fair
4) Left
5) Kid
6) Glasses
7) Rubber
8) Box
9) Still
10) Mind
11) Nail
12) Shoot
13) Mark
14) Cold
15) May
16) Fine
17) Grave
18) Sign
19) Ball
20) Match

---

1) Bill
2) Skip
3) Draw
4) Iris
5) Watch
6) Train
7) Stamp
8) Pupil
9) School
10) Fan
11) Wave
12) Lighter
13) Quiver
14) Even
15) Spring
16) Palm

PREFIX & SUFFIX

1) Comfortably
2) Crowded
3) Pronunciation
4) Economist
5) Handful
6) Mathematician
7) Tranquilize
8) Combination
9) Arrival
10) Intentions
11) Disappointment
12) Journalism
13) Inflation
14) Disastrous
15) Unorganized
16) Compromising
17) Familiarising
18) Reflection
19) Championship
20) Unsuccessful

---

1) Unable
2) Unbuttoned
3) Unload
4) Worthless
5) Regulate
6) Receptive
7) Surprisingly
8) Mistaken
9) Comedian
10) Employee
11) Widen
12) Uncompromising
13) Misplaced
14) Thoughtful
15) Frying
16) Worrying
17) Artist
18) Flowerist
19) Disobeys
20) Unfinished

IDIOMS

1) v
2) xii
3) iv
4) xi
5) xiii
6) xx
7) vii
8) xiv
9) vi
10) i
11) xv
12) xix
13) xvi
14) xviii
15) viii
16) ii
17) xvii
18) x
19) iii
20) ix

---

1) q
2) m
3) a
4) h
5) n
6) i
7) e
8) d
9) g
10) b
11) l
12) j
13) t
14) s
15) r
16) o
17) p
18) k
19) f

PHRASES

1) c
2) c
3) b
4) b
5) a
6) c
7) d
8) b
9) a
10) c
11) b
12) b
13) c
14) d
15) a
16) b
17) d
18) d
19) c
20) a

---

1) b
2) d
3) a
4) d
5) c
6) b
7) a
8) c
9) d
10) c
11) a
12) b
13) d
14) c
15) a
16) c
17) a
18) d
19) c
20) a

21) c
22) d
23) b
24) a
25) b
26) d
27) b
28) c
29) a
30) a
31) d
32) b
33) c
34) b
35) c

PROVERBS

1) ix
2) xii
3) ii
4) xv
5) xiv
6) v
7) xi
8) i
9) vii
10) xiii
11) x
12) viii
13) iii
14) iv
15) vi

---

1) vi
2) vii
3) i
4) viii
5) xiii
6) xv
7) iv
8) xviii
9) xvii
10) xvi
11) xiv
12) v
13) iii
14) x
15) ii
16) xii
17) xx
18) ix
19) xi
20) xix

ACRONYMS

1) Radio detection and Ranging
2) Navy, Army and Air Force Institutes
3) National Aeronautics and Space Administration
4) Light Amplification through Stimulated Emission of Radiation
5) Self-Contained Underwater Breathing Apparatus
6) United Nations Educational, Scientific and Cultural Organization
7) Acquired Immune Deficiency Syndrome
8) Scholastic Assessment Test
9) Personal Identification Number
10) Random Access Memory

---

1) Molecular Amplification by Stimulated Emission of Radiations
2) International Network
3) Sound navigation and ranging
4) Special Weapons and Tactics
5) Beginners All-purpose Symbolic Instruction Code
6) Basic Input/Output System
7) Association on Higher Education and Disability

8) Sequenced Transition to Education in the Public Schools
9) United Nations International Children's Emergency Fund.
10) United Nations Educational, Scientific and Cultural Organization

www.ingramcontent.com/pod-product-compliance
Lightning Source LLC
Chambersburg PA
CBHW070336230426
43663CB00011B/2343
9789350570807